A.K.A. JENNIFER GARNER

THE UNAUTHORIZED BIOGRAPHY OF AMERICA'S HOTTEST NEW STAR

A.K.A. JENNIFER GARNER

THE UNAUTHORIZED BIOGRAPHY OF
AMERICA'S HOTTEST NEW STAR

ibooks

Acknowledgments

My sincerest gratitude goes to Roger Cooper for being so passionate and, indeed, prescient, about Jennifer Garner. Without Roger, this book would not have been possible. And a big thank-you, Rog, for thinking of me to write it! Shawna Mullen, Christine Guarino Mayer, and Maria Tahim: you helped me immeasurably in the completion of the task. You are my heroes! Many thanks to the miracle worker J. Vita for an inspired and exciting design. Thanks as ever to the management and staff of the Omega Diner in Bayside, Queens, New York, for not kicking me and my laptop out into the street, and for always greeting me with a smile, no matter how sick of the sight of me you must be by now. I would also be remiss not to thank digital cable for the extensive film education it has provided me— even if all I thought I was doing was flaking off and procrastinating in all the time I've spent soak- ing in its many delightful offerings. Most of all, my heartfelt thanks goes to Francine Hornberger, who taught me everything I know about writing. Francine, you are my very voice.

For the "maenads": Maria, Christina, Stephanie, Colette, and Jen—
each a kick-ass Bond girl in her own right.

TABLE OF CONTENTS

A.K.A. JENNIFER GARNER

THE UNAUTHORIZED BIOGRAPHY OF
AMERICA'S HOTTEST NEW STAR

WARNING

HIGHLY CLASSIFIED
MATERIAL ENCLOSED

SUBJECT:
JENNIFER GARNER

Gorgeous Jennifer Garner is at the top of her career.

What's the biggest buzz these days at the office water cooler—or in the school cafeteria for that matter? Well it certainly isn't what just happened on Ally McBeal or ER. No, not anymore. Sure, shows like those still have their fair share of addicted viewers who religiously tune in every week. But, for the most part, the excitement that propels folks to work or school the morning after so they can eagerly pick apart each plot sequence and gush about the characters—that's pretty much died down by now.

These days, the most scintillating topic of discussion for the TV pop culture obsessed is the new ABC drama, Alias. Since its first commercial-free airing in September 2001, its intricate and involved plot lines and brilliantly acted characters have folks across America charged up and eager every Sunday night, bowls of popcorn at the ready. And after they are transported to a world of international espionage, cartoon-caliber action sequences, and the complicated interior life of the show's main character, Sydney Bristow, they are pretty much left foaming at the mouth for the next installment.

But behind the fascination with the show itself is the main reason audiences get glued to the TV when it airs. It's simple really. They are completely taken with the show's star, Jennifer Garner. Men and women alike. As Sydney the graduate student, Jennifer comes across as tormented and tentative. As the double agent, she is bold, brash, and brave. Jennifer pulls both off effortlessly—or so she makes it seem.

And this rampant enthrallment with Sydney—well it begs a huge question. Certainly one of the biggest pop culture wonders of our day and age is simple: Is actress Jennifer Garner just like the sexy, allusive, morally torn, impeccably dressed and shod double-agent, Sidney Bristow?

Most people are genuinely shocked when they learn about the real Jennifer. That she's not a femme fatale Hollywood glamour girl who's at the top of the A-list for all the big-name parties. That she's just an average gal who grew up in a semi-conservative Bible belt family.

And those fabulous moves she executes like a martial arts master—and yes, Jennifer does do most of her own stunts—the ones that look like she's been studying martial arts every since she stand up all by herself and toddle? Well, Jennifer only started to learn them just one short month before she auditioned for the role that would make her a star.

THE REAL JENNIFER HAS NO BURNING DESIRE FOR THE SPOTLIGHT—AT LEAST NOT FOR THE TYPICAL TRAPPINGS OF MEGA-STARDOM. SHE'S A PERENNIAL HOMEBODY WHO'D RATHER SNUGGLE UP AT HOME WITH HUBBY SCOTT FOLEY, WATCHING BOB VILLA RE-RUNS, THAN HIT THE TOWN FOR A NIGHT OF FLASH AND SPARKLE AND RUBBING ELBOWS WITH TOP HOLLYWOOD LUMINARIES.

In fact, following the 2002 Golden Globes, from which Jennifer went home with a statue for her work in Alias, there was an after party. She and Scott attended, but only briefly. They ducked out almost right away, racing home to get out of their formalwear, and left so early in fact that they were able to catch the TV broadcast of the event from their own living room.

"We were out of there so fast," she admitted to Time magazine. Jennifer Garner is not a social butterfly. "When we got to the party, people started coming up to me, and I felt, 'I just don't belong here.'" She was glad when they ducked out. "We felt like we had gotten away with something big," she chuckled.

No, unlike Sydney, Jennifer does not wear formalwear like it's a second skin. Beautiful in an understated way, Jennifer much prefers wearing jeans and cargo pants with comfy sneakers to the outrageous outfits Sydney dons—or the fashionable shoes she spikes around in.

And yet, **SYDNEY IS A ROLE THAT JENNIFER PULLS OFF MAGNIFICENTLY. SHE'S A MEGA-TALENT AND A PERFECTIONIST WHO IMPRESSES EVERYONE WHO WORKS WITH HER—IT DOESN'T MATTER HOW LONG THE STINT.**

And her costars appreciate that she is the main reason that Alias has become such a hit show. "She's the reason the show's working," Victor Garber, who plays Sydney's allusive father, Jack Bristow. "There's a kind of sadness underneath Jennifer's incredibly jovial exterior—more an awareness of sadness in the world. She gets that, and in that way she's very close to Sydney."

After acting against Jennifer for an episode of Alias, rouge film director Quentin Tarantino was simply blown away by her talent. "Week in and week out, Jennifer is doing fights

So in love... Jennifer and husband Scott Foley met on the set of Felicity, **and it's been magic ever since.**

in tight rubber dresses and heels, so, really, props," he reported to Rolling Stone. "And at the same time she's doing all of this dramatic stuff." This means a lot coming from a director who could turn Vinnie Barbarino (a.k.a. John Travolta) into convincing killer Vincent Vega in Pulp Fiction. Tarantino knows talent and versatility when he sees it, and he sees it in Jennifer Garner. "When I met her, I said, 'Just so you know, you're gonna work forever,'" he told Rolling Stone. "You don't have to prove nothin' to nobody no more.'"

And he's not alone in that sentiment. Jennifer Garner has shot up from general actress obscurity to being the brightest

Jennifer and Scott at the 28th Annual People's Choice Awards.

new face on television—not to mention countless magazine covers. With all the attention Mrs. Scott Foley has been getting in recent months, there's no question that her star is on the rise—and even in the intergalactic realm she's reached, the entire universe is still expanding to contain her magic.

But everyone who knows her knows that superstardom won't go to her head. She's insanely grounded and stable. "She's 29. She's had a lot of time to not work," Alias creator and producer J.J. Abrams told USA Today in a recent interview. "She's a married woman. She had a down-to-earth family. She's not 19 and new to town. She's a real human being with a real solid perspective."

And Jennifer has no arguments with this perception of her. She embraces it. "What I'm fine at is fitting in whatever situation I find myself in," she told Time magazine. "If I'm the fifth lead in a huge movie, I'm happy. If I'm in the foreground, I'm happy saying, 'O.K., this is my job, and I have to do this.'"

She may be accommodating, but she's anything but boring. Think of Jennifer Garner as the nice girl with an edge; the girl next door packing heat—if only in character.

And Jennifer pulls her off masterfully. So who exactly is the babe behind the brawn? Read on and see!

Maggie Marron

—Maggie Marron

A.K.A. JENNIFER GARNER

THE UNAUTHORIZED BIOGRAPHY OF
AMERICA'S HOTTEST NEW STAR

YOU CAN CALL ME JAN

CHAPTER ONE

"I DEFINITELY HAVE THE MIDDLE-CHILD THING OF 'GIVE ME ATTENTION!'"

—JENNIFER GARNER TO ROLLING STONE MAGAZINE

What kind of childhood does a future star of TV and film have? Typically, it's one marked by being dragged back and forth to auditions, waking up hours before school starts to head to song and dance classes, and giving up all the normal enjoyments of youth—including, sometimes, being taught by tutors instead of attending a regular school because the demands of their professional schedule can't permit the time.

HOW DID THE WOMAN WHO WOULD BECOME THE MOST FAMOUS INTERNATIONAL SPY IN THE WORLD GROW UP?

Not like this. Not entirely.

She did dream that maybe she might be a spy one day—one of the many ambitions Jennifer Garner had growing up.

"MY FAVORITE BOOK WAS HARRIET THE SPY,"

she told Entertainment Weekly. "I probably read it 10 times. I talked my mom into buying me a little notebook like Harriet the Spy had. And I'd write down these things about my neighbors. 'Marge is wearing polka dots today. She has a poodle. Both start with "P." Think about that.' I so truly wanted to be a spy," she laughed.

But aside from the neighborhood espionage, Jennifer Garner's childhood was utterly average. Born in Houston, Texas, her family moved to Charleston, West Virginia, for her dad's job. There, the Garner family settled.

Charleston is the state capital, but a small town by the standards of most large cities. Charleston has a population of about

60,000. Compare that to Boston, with 600,000. Or Seattle—900,000. Manhattan has a population of 1.5 million+, and Los Angeles—a whopping 3.5 million.

SO JENNIFER GREW UP WITH A DIFFERENT PERSPECTIVE THAN MOST STARLETS WHO EVENTUALLY END UP IN HOLLYWOOD. IT'S NOT THAT SHE'S SHELTERED; IT'S THAT SHE ISN'T JADED.

"I'm all about growing up in West Virginia," Jennifer relayed in an interview on Entertainment Tonight. "It's the most beautiful place in the world. It's such an isolated community where you're not affected by cities and trends. We're lucky to have the Limited and Lane Bryant."

The daughter of Pat, a college English professor, and Bill, a chemical engineer, Jennifer had a modest and wholesome Christian upbringing. She is the middle of three girls, and has admitted on more than one occasion to having had a classic "Jan Brady" complex. Her older sister, Melissa, was a tough act to follow. She was high school valedictorian, a piano prodigy, and a champion majorette—among several other talents. (Marcia! Marcia! Marcia!) And then there's Susannah, the baby of the family.

But Jennifer didn't disappear in her family just because she was the middle child. The family got along just fine. All the girls got along, shared clothes, and never fought—okay, maybe sometimes!

And she didn't disappear in the town either. She was a budding entrepreneur in high school, working at everything from mowing lawns to babysitting. "She was very much known here," Jennifer's mother Pat fondly remembered to Rolling Stone. "She must have babysat half of Charleston."

Yes, the Garner girls were typical girls who went to dances and the mall. They hung out with friends, but essentially stayed out of trouble. And all grown up, all of the girls are successful in their careers, nary a neurosis among them. Why? Jennifer completely acknowledges her parents' role in it. "My mom had all these rules to make us well rounded," she told Rolling Stone. "She didn't push us much. It was more like success, doing good was just quietly expected."

But just because her parents didn't push her didn't mean that Jennifer didn't push herself.

EVER SINCE SHE WAS A LITTLE GIRL, JENNIFER WAS ALWAYS STRIVING TO DO EVERYTHING SHE SET HER MIND TO IN THE BEST WAY SHE COULD.

But we'll come back to that.

The Garners weren't wealthy, but they did their best to provide their girls with anything they could. But the best gift that Pat and Bill Garner gave their daughters, however, was to teach them to be resourceful and always do the best with what they had. None of the girls was ever spoiled. "We didn't have any

EVEN IN BOOKWORM MODE, JENNIFER IS SIMPLY BREATHTAKING!

money," Jennifer told Seventeen magazine, "so we learned from our mother to rotate our outfits. Mom had three: her day-to-day gear, her church best and her gardening clothes."

There was no such thing as mine! mine! mine! in the Garner household. All the girls were taught to share with one another and to be grateful for what they had. But because of the differences in ages, sometimes the sharing of clothes could result in one or two fashion nightmares. As Jennifer remembered for Seventeen magazine: "My sophomore year I went to the prom in this enormous hoopskirt that my sister wore three years earlier. You had to lift it to fit through the door," she laughed. "All the other girls were wearing chic little dresses. It was horrifying."

Horrifying, yes. But devastating—nah. Jennifer bounced back pretty quickly from that. Even back then, when most girls her age would vow to never show her face in school ever again, she was too grounded to let anything throw her off too badly.

Jennifer moved through school on even keel. She didn't get the straight A's that Melissa did (Marcia! Marcia! Marcia!), but she still got by with B's and B plusses.

SHE WAS A SERIOUS STUDENT, AND WHEN SHE WASN'T READING FOR SCHOOL, YOU COULD PRETTY MUCH GUARANTEE THAT JENNIFER WOULD HAVE HER NOSE BURIED IN SOME BOOK OR OTHER.

All of that reading has given her a great vocabulary, and on top of coming across as sweet, unpretentious, and down to earth in interviews, she also comes off sounding witty and clever. Some girls just seem to have it all!

Jennifer had her own friends, but it's a safe guess you won't find her name if you looked it up in the popularity polls in her high school yearbook. "I wasn't popular," she told Seventeen, "but I wasn't tragic either."

When she wasn't in classes, Jennifer spent her time throughout high school doing laps with the swim team, playing the saxophone in the high school band, and by continuing the ballet lessons she had started as a small girl. (Jennifer Garner actually took twelve years of ballet lessons, which makes it more than a small wonder that she can pull off strappy sandals like she can. Most ballet dancers totally wreck their feet by spending all that time up on their toes. Jennifer seems no worse for the wear.)

Jennifer had her share of boyfriends, but there was no one true love who really swept her off her feet too dramatically in high school. Which is not to say that she didn't fall in love in high school, either. She most certainly did—but it was not with a boy.

IT WAS IN HIGH SCHOOL THAT JENNIFER WOULD DISCOVER THE PASSION THAT WOULD TAKE HER RIGHT TO THE TOP.

One day, she happened to wander into the drama club. Despite how much time she spent practicing ballet, she realized she was probably never going to be good enough to hit the big time. So for the rest of her high school career, she acted. (Though she didn't give up her ballet lessons until she went away to college.)

Jennifer was very dedicated, but she never had any idea she would grow up to be a star. It just wasn't what you thought about growing up in West Virginia. "I was so committed to dance. I danced six hours every day. I wasn't even a very good dancer, to be honest," she admitted to Entertainment Tonight. "I went to college and I saw I could major in theater and keep learning about it. I didn't know where I

could take it, but I knew I had to do it."

And thank goodness she did.

IT'S HARD TO IMAGINE ANY OTHER ACTRESS PULLING OFF SYDNEY BRISTOW BETTER THAN JENNIFER GARNER.

So how do her parents feel about their daughter's new rise to fame—and all the crazy things Jennifer does on screen every week? "Our local newspaper called and said what did I think about Alias, how in the first episode she gets tortured and has her tooth pulled out," Pat Garner told Rolling Stone. "I said, 'Well, I hate to see her tortured, but we've seen her raped, we've seen her killed, we've seen her abort, so what's a tooth?'"

Playful or not, Jennifer's parents are extremely proud of all their daughters. And while they may worry about her and the stunts in which she partakes for her job, they know that how she got there was through hard work and determination—two qualities that carried her right through high school and straight into college.

TOP SECRET INFORMATION
FOR YOUR EYES ONLY

VITAL STATISTICS

JENNIFER GARNER VITAL STATISTICS

DATE OF BIRTH: APRIL 17, 1972

STAR SIGN: ARIES

BIRTHPLACE: HOUSTON, TEXAS

HOMETOWN: CHARLESTON, WEST VIRGINIA

PARENTS: PAT AND BILL GARNER

SISTERS: MELISSA (OLDER) AND
              SUSANNAH (YOUNGER)

PETS: TWO DOGS—CHARLIE ROSE AND
              MAGGIE MAY

HUSBAND: SCOTT FOLEY (NOEL ON FELICITY)

NOTABLE ROLES: SYDNEY BRISTOW ON ALIAS
              HANNAH ON FELICITY
              WANDA IN DUDE, WHERE'S MY CAR?

PET PEEVE: DRUNKS

WHAT'S IN A

Jennifer Garner is a bright star in her own right—but what do the stars reveal about this heavenly Aries? Her April 17 birthday puts her in the sign of the Ram, but just barely. Her star chart shows a dedicated nature that is willing to make sacrifices in order to keep things running smoothly. This sounds like tenacious Jennifer, who admits to being a homebody who loves to cook, yet shines in each physically demanding episode of the show: "I've been drowned, hit with a gun, chased in a car,

STAR SIGN?

and hung by a wire from a 13-story building," she laughs.

Aries is a fire sign, which explains a lot of Jen's spark in creating her TV personality Sydney Bristow. So do these other Aries traits: courage, generosity, strength, and an outgoing, dynamic nature. But there is a softer side of Aries, too. Jennifer's stars suggest a personality that loves to improve the home. Her chart also shows that she is someone who needs to have a pleasant environment in order to be happy.

People with her birthday are supposed to have the gift of making unique events transpire. They are also meant to excel in unusual careers—be that an actress or a double agent!

RUSSELL CROWE

SARAH JESSICA PARKER

A/K/A: JENNIFER GARNER. JACKMAN WEEKS

KATE HUDSON

Other Celebrity Aries include

Sarah Jessica Parker (March 25)
Robert Downey, Jr. (April 4)
Russell Crowe (April 7)
Mandy Moore (April 10)
Sarah Michelle Gellar (April 14)
Kate Hudson (April 19)

A/K/A: JENNIFER GARNER

TEST YOUR JENNIFER IQ
PART ONE

THINK YOU KNOW ALL THERE IS TO KNOW ABOUT THE CHILDHOOD OF *ALIAS* STAR JENNIFER GARNER? SURE, SOME ANSWERS COME RIGHT OUT OF THIS CHAPTER, SO IF YOU WERE READING CLOSELY, YOU SHOULD DO FINE. AND THAT DOESN'T MEAN YOU SHOULD PEEK BACK TO THE CHAPTER FOR THE ANSWERS—SEE WHAT YOU CAN REMEMBER ON YOUR OWN! WHEN YOU'RE DONE WITH THE QUIZ, BE SURE TO TURN TO THE BACK OF THE BOOK AND WRITE IN YOUR SCORE. AND GOOD LUCK!

1) What town was Jennifer was born in?
   a. Charleston, West Virginia
   b. Philadelphia, Pennsylvania
   c. Houston, Texas
   d. Wilmington, Delaware

2) What's Jennifer's mother's name?
   a. Sally
   b. Pat
   c. Freida
   d. Annabelle

3) How many brothers does Jennifer have?
   a. one
   b. two
   c. three
   d. none

4) How many years of ballet lessons did Jennifer take?
   a. four
   b. six
   c. twelve
   d. she still takes ballet to this day

5) What jobs did Jennifer do growing up to make extra money?
   a. mowed lawns
   b. delivered papers
   c. babysat
   d. all of the above

A.K.A. JENNIFER GARNER

THE UNAUTHORIZED BIOGRAPHY OF
AMERICA'S HOTTEST NEW STAR

CHASING DOWN A DREAM

CHAPTER TWO

"I GUESS I DON'T SEE ANY REAL REASON NOT TO BE IN CONTROL."

—JENNIFER GARNER TO *ROLLING STONE*

After Jennifer graduated high school, she headed to Denison University in Ohio to earn a bachelors degree for drama.

JENNIFER TOOK HER STEADFASTLY SERIOUS SELF RIGHT ALONG TO COLLEGE WITH HER.

Some kids use going to college and finally getting away from home as an excuse to act crazy and do things they would never do while living with their parents. Not Jennifer, though. She kept her nose decidedly clean.

Which is not to say she was completely boring either. She was in a sorority, after all. Although this affiliation might as well have been for appearances only, as Jennifer hardly ever took an active part in the social aspect of the sisterhood. Especially not the party-till-you-drop aspect of it.

Mostly, this is exactly what she wanted to do.

SCHOOL WAS A PLACE THAT SHE WAS GOING TO TAKE SERIOUSLY. TUITION WASN'T EXACTLY FREE, AND SHE, AS SHE WAS RAISED, WAS NOT ABOUT TO FLIT AWAY HER PARENT'S HARD-EARNED MONEY AT VARIOUS KEG PARTIES

No, she was there to help herself become someone, to do something important with her life. For Jennifer, parties were little more than a distraction.

Sometimes she regrets this, however, as once you leave college, you don't ever quite have that freedom to be so reckless ever again. "I used to wish I could go back and do college again," she told Rolling Stone, "take away some of the drive, have a little more fun, get drunk, experiment—that kind of stuff."

But if the regret is there, it's only in passing. By the time she got to college, Jennifer had become very serious about her acting. No longer enclosed in the safe confines of her close-knit West Virginian community, she started to think that perhaps there might be a future for her on stage or screen.

Whatever the outcome, the dedication would have been the same.

JENNIFER GENERALLY DIVIDED HER TIME BETWEEN AUDITIONING FOR ROLES, PLAYING ROLES, AND READING SCRIPTS FOR AUDITIONS FOR UPCOMING ROLES.

"You couldn't drag me away from the drama department," she told Seventeen magazine.

Even today, Jennifer has not succumbed to the trappings of the celebrity lifestyle. Rather, she is happier focusing on the things that matter to her most, whether that means staying at home, kicking back and watching TV, or working as much as her body and mind can possibly withstand. She's not much for the social scene, just like she was back then. "I didn't like parties and I still don't."

It's not that Jennifer is antisocial. She's just never been into partying. Drugs have never even been a consideration for her, and drinking she limits to enjoying a nice bottle of red wine over dinner with husband Scott Foley. Not only is she not into drinking, in fact, she actually strongly dislikes drunken people: "I just feel really sorry for them," she told Rolling Stone. "They're so uncontrolled and gross and sweaty and about to puke."

Summers she spent in Atlanta, Georgia, doing summer stock. In

JENNIFER WAS ALWAYS WORKING— EVEN WHILE SHE WAS STILL IN COLLEGE

Atlanta, she received probably the worst advice of her entire career— and perhaps life. During one of the productions, an unnamed New York theater veteran, who was decidedly unimpressed by Jennifer's talent, told Jennifer that she should forget acting and change her major completely in school. That she should take classes that would earn her a paralegal or some such similar degree.

Jennifer Garner, paralegal. Nope. This was not something a determined Jennifer Garner took lightly. No-sir-ee! "I wanted to take her down," Jennifer told Movieline.com. Were shades of Sydney starting to surface even back then? You have to wonder what size foot that expert theater veteran is choking on now!

Summer stock launched new opportunities for Jennifer. Before even graduating from college, Jennifer had managed to land a small part in 1990 episode of Law & Order. No paralegal degree—but a part on a law show! Oh yes. That would suit her just fine.

Right after she graduated college in 1994, Jennifer had to make a choice. Would she move back to her beloved and secure hometown, or would she take a chance on the rest of the world and see what kind of potential she had to offer.

Jennifer decided that while Charleston would always be home, she was not going to make it her home. Not at this time.

IT WAS TIME TO SPREAD HER WINGS AS AN ACTRESS AND SEEK OUT OPPORTUNITIES WHERE SHE COULD READILY FIND THEM.

Community theater was simply not going to do the trick. So she headed to New York.

In the Big Apple, Jennifer did as much theater as she possibly could do. One of the first gigs she landed was a role as an understudy for the Broadway production of A Month in the Country. And Jennifer was still the same Jennifer. Reportedly, while the other understudies hung out in the dressing rooms, giggling and gossiping about the stars, Jennifer watched each and every performance from the wings. She spent her time studying the stars and learning from them as she watched them in action, while she soaked up the reactions of the audience to the various performances.

Showing just how small a world show business is, and how at least a version of the famous game, "Six Degrees of Kevin Bacon" can be applicable to any celebrity, one of the stars of this particular show was Ron Rifkin. Already an established performer, he would receive a Tony Award a few years later for his

Ron Rifkin at the premiere of The Negotiator in 1998.

performance in Cabaret. And a few years after that, he would be cast as Arvin Sloane, in a supporting role on the show of which Jennifer

WHEN JENNIFER HAD GOTTEN AS MUCH EXPERIENCE AS SHE COULD FROM NEW YORK, SHE WAS SOON ON HER WAY TO LOS ANGELES TO PURSUE FILM AND TV PARTS.

Jennifer on break from taping Alias.

would be the star: Alias, of course!

Her first break came when she was cast as Melissa Gilbert's daughter in Zoya, a made-for-TV movie based on the novel by Danielle Steele.

The year 1996 was a big TV year for Jennifer. She clinched another spot on Law & Order. And then she appeared on The Pretender and had an opportunity got to test out her comic mettle when she was cast in an episode of Spin City.

In 1996, she also got wonderful reviews for her performance in Rose Hill, the Hallmark Hall of Fame made-for-TV adaptation of Julie Garwood's best-selling novel, For the Roses.

Between jobs, Jennifer was unemployed a lot—as much as the next actor—but she never gave up. She started to feel like if she just held out, her big break would eventually come.

For Jennifer, the next year would be for movies what 1996 had been for TV. She finally broke out onto the big screen, but in teeny tiny bit parts. She was even cast in the Woody Allen film Deconstructing Harry, an honor and an "arrival" for any actor. Of course, her part was so small, billed only as "woman in elevator," that if you blink you'll probably miss her!

She had larger roles in Mr. Magoo, starring Leslie Nielson, and Washington Square, starring Jennifer Jason Leigh and Albert Finney, but they were never large or significant enough to warrant mention on movie posters or even be considered in film reviews.

Still, she was expanding her skills and getting exposure.

IF YOU WATCH ANY OF THOSE EARLY MOVIES NOW, AFTER KNOWING WHO SHE IS, THERE'S NO QUESTION THAT JENNIFER HAS APPEARED ON THE SCREEN. HER PRESENCE IS LARGE—NO MATTER HOW SMALL THE PART

And this is one of the most common things anyone who works with Jennifer knows.

SHE COMMANDS EACH AND EVERY ROLE LIKE SHE WAS BORN TO PLAY IT.

And this is the exact quality that allowed for her to be cast in Alias. But we'll get into that later.

By 1998, Jennifer started to get roles that made her more than just a glorified extra. But it would still be three more long years until she would become a star.

"Hmmm ... that's a very interesting point."

THE KICK-ASS BABES HALL OF FAME

Part of what makes Sydney Bristow one of the most interesting femme fighters—big and small screen alike—is the dimension with which Jennifer portrays the character. Here are some more multidimensional butt-kicking babes.

A/K/A: JENNIFER GARNER THE REAL STORY

ANGELINA JOLIE AS LARA CROFT IN *TOMB RAIDER*

If anyone could bring the pre- and post-pubescent male videogame nut's dream character to life on the big screen, it was real-life badass Angelina Jolie.

Like Sydney Bristow, Lara Croft also leads a double life: she is a well-groomed British aristocrat who collects antiquities, but who must learn martial arts and other combat skills so that she can stop a precious artifact from falling into the hands of an evil organization.

Angelina Jolie's character was so badass, it inspired its very own action figure!

CAMERON DIAZ, DREW BARRYMORE, AND LUCY LIU FROM *CHARLIE'S ANGELS.*

Just like real superheroes hailing from the Hall of Justice, these gorgeous babes save the world—and are the ideal mix of glam, grit, and gusto. Producer Barrymore didn't want the Angels to use guns—which actually worked out better for the film. The cowardly bad guys shot at the Angels, who flipped and kicked and punched their way out off peril.

The Angels strut their stuff at the Charlie's Angels premiere at Mann's Chinese Theater in October 2000.

A/K/A: JENNIFER GARNER THE REAL STORY

SARAH MICHELLE GELLAR AS BUFFY THE VAMPIRE SLAYER.

Like Sydney, Buffy is a regular student by fashion, but a pawn of justice by fate. Born into her slayer legacy, Buffy proves beyond a shadow of a doubt that tiny blondes should be taken very seriously.

KRISTY SWANSON AS THE ORIGINAL BUFFY (FILM VERSION)

The cheerleader with killer cramps fights against her nemeses Rutger Hauer and side-kick Paul Reubens (a.k.a. Pee Wee Herman) as the latest in generations of vampire slayers. Guided by trainer Donald Sutherland, she playfully roundhouse kicks vampire butt—those kicks significantly improved by years of cheerleader practices—and rescues, more than once, love interest Luke Perry.

JESSICA ALBA AS MAX IN DARK ANGEL

In Terminator-director James Cameron's first foray into small-screen action and suspense, petite powerhouse Max is a genetically enhanced human with super-human powers. Her mission is to find others like her and to bring down the organization that turned them into mutants.

Jessica Alba, the Dark Angel herself, presents an award with Jennifer at the 53rd Annual Emmy Awards in November 2001.

A/K/A: JENNIFER GARNER THE REAL STORY

BRIDGET FONDA AS MAGGIE (CODE NAME: NINA), IN POINT OF NO RETURN

She started out on the wrong side of the law as a psychopathic cop killer with a passion for illicit pharmaceuticals. But a staged execution brings Maggie into a world of conspiracy and intrigue as a hired assassin who is forced to kill to keep herself alive—and get her life back—all while she begins to develop a crazy little thing like a conscience. Maggie learns to "never much mind the little things" and pulls it all off in killer outfits and heels.

LYNDA CARTER AS WONDER WOMAN

Wonder Woman started the trend for beautiful and busty women to kick prodigious amounts of evildoers' butts on television. She proved that you could pull off wearing a cleavage-revealing, push-up, sparkly, yet patriotic leotard and still keep your hair in place and gold tiara firmly secured.

There's a lot of competition out there for the number-one slot, but Jennifer's not threatened. "Buffy has supernatural powers, the Dark Angel is genetically altered, and Lara Croft has those guns in her socks," she told *Esquire.* "But mano a mano? If it was just fists and kicks? I'd say they have to get up pretty early."

Jennifer Garner spots a Neve Campbell–type pixie cut for the Scream premiere in Westwood, California.

41

BEHIND THE MOVES

If you're like most fans of Alias, you no doubt sit back in awe watching Sydney pulverize her enemies each and every week. Jennifer had to take lots of lessons to look as good as she does in full fighting mode—but she admits that she does have a stunt double, Olympic gold medallist Dana Hee, who executes the really hairy moves. Want to follow what Sydney's doing when she's kicking serious subversive butt? Here are some of the basics.

Jab:
The most basic punch. This one comes right from the front of the body and most of the weight is on the front foot. It involves pushing the arm in a straight line from the knuckles, and moves as if punching right through the target. It's great for hitting just below the nose, the Solar Plexis, temple, or carotid artery.

Hook:
In this punch, the weight of the body is also on the front leg. The punching arm is at a 90-degree angle with the body—the arm should look as if resting on a wall. To execute the punch, the upper body twists to make contact with the opposite side of the attacker's body (a left hook will get the attacker's right side). Its most effective targets: the jaw, ribs, and nose.

Uppercut:
This move packs a wallop at the jaw, face, or chest of the opponent. It starts from behind the hip and moves up through the front of the body, extending knees as you come up. The body's weight is on the opposite leg of the punching arm.

Cross punch (also known as "power punch"):
The most powerful of punches, this one comes from behind and derives its power as the hips and the shoulder also become part of the punch—not just the arm. Targets for this punch are the Solar Plexis and just below the nose.

Elbow strike:
This cool little maneuver is the perfect badass move for finishing off—an up-close and powerful strike. To execute this move, bend your arm, turn your back foot and shift your weight onto it. Strike with the front of the elbow. Great for getting temple, jaws, cheekbone, and neck targets.

Front kick:
Always gorgeously executed by Sydney with all the grace of a Radio City Music Hall Rockette. For this kick, all the weight moves onto the rear leg. The front leg, the kicking leg, is raised with a bent knee, and then the foot snaps up from the knee. The target—shins, just below the kneecaps, groin, and, if you can really kick high, the chin, gets slammed with the ball of the foot.

Side kick:
This is a total power kick that involves kicking with the heel. All the weight gets shifted to the resting leg. The kicking leg, with bent knee, lines up in front of the body, foot flexed and aimed sideward. The target gets hit with the heel, not the top, of the foot. Great for knocking out shins, kneecaps, and groins.

Roundhouse kick:
A roundhouse kick is a lot like a sidekick, but this time, instead of kicking with the heel, the target gets nailed with the front of the foot. Really lays it into the side of the kneecap, the side of the thigh, and the side of the abdomen.

Back kick:
Also like the sidekick—but perfect for sneaky attackers. All the weight of the body shifts to resting leg, which is slightly bent. Kick out back leg with heel, making sure to keep your eye on the target: an evil groin, hip, or kneecap.

Drop kick:
A beauty of a kick that starts with one knee—not the one on the kicking leg—raised. When the knee drops, the other leg simultaneously executes a high front kick. The momentum gives the kick more power and the kicker greater balance. Targets the groin, hip, kneecap, or chin.

SECRET WORD DECODER MISSION

```
W C G M A L A P O D N O W K E A T F A R
R I O P Y K I I D X A S O S H L E S M E
E H L B O I O T C H M O M N S P Y R C M
N C O T Z R O B R A H L R A E P C E O C
R R B W O T S I R B Y E N D I S L H L O
A P L A A N G B F E N V I M R E L T F L
G C I L L P A V L N L K A Y R B S O T F
R D H I A J W O M F L R R T X O Y T L E
E G S A J W F C M B T O L I S L B N C L
F O R S R T A O N H R S K C L G R A I C
I E M N T L T K A R A E G I H N O C I D
N R F O P G E S B I A H O L Y E V I O D
U C C R P T S S A Y I Z E H D K F D U O
E S Q A A E U I T N L L M F W L C I H H
J P H I W C R B Y O I L D L A O C N U U
L C L A Y W T M D P N S E C E G N G N N
D L R P U A N N A H W I Y T C A A I I I
F T I M E O F Y O U R L I F E F H S G G
T N E G A E L B U O D M E F L P A U T
```

SECRET WORD DECODER MISSION

HOW GOOD A SECRET AGENT WOULD YOU MAKE? NOW IT'S TIME TO PLAY YOUR OWN LITTLE SPY GAME. WORDS RELATING TO JENNIFER GARNER AND ALIAS HAVE BEEN CRAFTILY HIDDEN AWAY IN THE FOLLOWING PUZZLE. SEE IF YOU HAVE WHAT IT TAKES TO SOLVE IT!

(THE ANSWER KEY APPEARS ON PAGE 112—BUT NO CHEATING!)

HIDDEN WORDS

ALIAS

BALLET

CHARLESTON

CIA

DOUBLE AGENT

FELICITY

GOLDEN GLOBES

HANNA

JJ ABRAMS

JENNIFER GARNER

MARTHA STEWART

PEARL HARBOR

ROSE HILL

SCOTT FOLEY

SIDNEY BRISTOW

SIGNIFICANT

OTHERS

SPY

TAE KWON DO

TIME OF YOUR LIFE

ZOYA

TEST YOUR JENNIFER IQ
PART TWO

So now you're back for more? You made it through the first round, and now you're ready for your next challenge, eh? How much do you know about Level 2 of Jennifer's life? About her college years and early part of her career? Well there's only one way to find out! Take the second part of the quiz, natch! And when you're done, don't forget to turn to the back of the book and write in your score. And good luck!

1) Where did Jennifer go to college?
    a. Denison University in Ohio
    b. The University of West Virginia
    c. Adelphi University in New York
    d. Tulane University in New Orleans

2) What was the name of the show Jennifer appeared in with Ron Rifkin?
    a. Cabaret
    b. Month in the Country
    c. The Alchemist
    d. Hedda Gabler

3) What sit-com did Jennifer make an appearance on?
    a. Just Shoot Me
    b. Friends
    c. Frasier
    d. Spin City

4) Which former child TV actress played Jennifer's mom in Zoya?
    a. Dana Plato
    b. Candace Cameron
    c. Melissa Gilbert
    d. Tracy Gold

5. Which big-name filmmaker gave Jennifer a tiny role in his film Deconstructing Harry?
    a. James Cameron
    b. Woody Allen
    c. Robert Altman
    d. John Hughes

Jennifer and hubby Scott Foley at the 12th
Annual Kids' Choice Awards in 1999.

A/K/A: JENNIFER GARNER THE REAL STORY

HIGHS AND LOWS

CHAPTER THREE

"I KNEW I WAS GREAT IN *DUDE, WHERE'S MY CAR?*, BUT SERIOUSLY!"

—JENNIFER GARNER UPON RECEIVING THE GOLDEN GLOBE FOR BEST ACTRESS IN A TV SERIES, DRAMA

On Sunday nights, ABC broadcasts two top shows: Alias and The Practice. Both shows were dreamed up and written in part by fairly young men who have established themselves as masters of innovative television. But there's another common bond. The Practice features actress Marla Sokoloff in its stellar cast. Alias, well we know whom Alias stars. So what's the connection, you may ask?

Well, here's another example of just how small a world Hollywood is: Garner and Sokoloff acted together in the first film in which Garner had any real presence at all: Dude, Where's My Car? The giant-ish Jennifer and the minute Marla made for quite a charming duo as "the twins," the girlfriends of the film's two stars, That 70's Show's Ashton Kutcher and Seann William Scott. But that would come later.

Jennifer is escorted on the arm of her Dude, Where's My Car? co-star Ashton Kutcher to the film's premiere.

JENNIFER WORKED MORE IN 1998 THAN SHE EVER HAD BEFORE. IT WOULD ALSO BE A YEAR MARKED WITH TURNING POINTS: AT LEAST TWO VERY SIGNFICANT ONES.

Jennifer started the year with a role on the short-lived ABC series remake of Fantasy Island, which starred Malcolm McDowell as the ever-allusive Mr. Rourke. Jennifer played her role well, but the

Keri Russel, the star of Felicity

memory of her having acted it is about as vague for TV viewers as that there was ever a remake of Fantasy Island.

Next, she made her first of two appearances on the WB's breakthrough hit show, Felicity. She played the vile Hanna, Noel's ex-girlfriend, who had come back into his life and was desperately trying to keep Noel away from Felicity. Jennifer made a big splash, but not necessarily in a positive way. Not to fans of Keri Russell's passionately adored character.

In an interview with E! Online, Jennifer admitted that there was considerable back-lash with fans of the show. "I'm hated," she chuckled. "I'm hated on the Internet; I'm hated on the streets. People constantly come up to me and say 'I hate Hanna.' And I say, 'Well, I married [Scott], so I don't know what else to tell you.' At first I took it personally. Then I was like, Jennifer, get over yourself."

Remarkably, even though she did such an amazing job that she raised the ire of television watchers across the nation, it actually took more than one audition for Jennifer to land this role. How about five? And no, that isn't a joke. Just ask Jennifer: "J.J. [Abrams] made me audition five times for that," she told USA Today. "For a guest spot. For one episode." One wonders if Abrams wasn't trying to get a better sense of the actress as he germinated in his head his next creation— even if he didn't know it yet. Maybe all those auditions even inspired him on some level. Hey, you never know!

Jennifer would make two appearances on the show in 1998.

And in between, she got what she believed was going to be her break-through role. Chris Keyser and Amy Littman were developing their next series after the runaway success of their family drama, Party of Five. They came up with a concept: Three single twentysomethings deal with the pressures of being out of school, being grown up, and making it in the big, bad adult world.

Jennifer was cast to play Nell, a young woman trudging through her mid-twenties with her two best male friends on either arm. While Nell becomes sexually involved with one of the guys, which strains the friendship for the threesome, she can never truly decide what it is she

SHE'S FLIGHTY AND FLAKY AND UNSTABLE — A REAL STRETCH FOR JENNIFER. THOUGH JENNIFER'S ACTING EFFORTS, SADLY, WERE NOT APPRECIATED BY CRITICS AND VIEWERS ALIKE, WHO JUST COULDN'T SEEM TO APPRECIATE POOR NELL.

wants from life.

Mainly, she was scorned and her character, and everything that had to do with the show, despised.

For a less talented actress, the role may have meant career suicide. Especially because of the brutality with which reviewers attacked the show and its cast. After viewing Significant Others, Ken Tucker of Entertainment Weekly wrote of her performance: "Jennifer Garner's Nell is all perky superficiality—I realize that she's supposed to be a neurotic nice girl who can't decide what to do with her life, but the way Garner plays her, Nell is almost clinically schizo: zippy and enthusiastic

Scott and Jennifer attend a GQ **magazine party at The Factory Space in Westwood, California, February 2001.**

BUT JENNIFER DIDN'T LET THAT ONE GET HER DOWN EITHER. SHE HAD MORE STUFF TO LOOK FORWARD TO — OF THIS SHE WAS SURE.

one second, mopey and despairing the next."

(Interestingly enough, years later, when Jennifer would become Sydney Bristow, Tucker wouldn't forget this show, but he would give her the credit she deserved: "Garner is exceptionally adroit as Sydney; previously confined to short-lived series...and bit parts in major cinematic events...she's a full-blown star with acting chops [in Alias]."

Significant Others was universally panned, and whisked off the air quicker than you can say unemployment line. It was a disappointment, but Jennifer at least had another appearance on Felicity to look forward to that year.

Lippman and Keyser hadn't forgotten about their hapless female star, so in 1999, when they developed Time of Your Life, the Party of Five spin-off-slash-Jennifer Love Hewitt vehicle, they pulled Garner in to play Hewitt's sidekick, an aspiring actress named Romy Sullivan.

But alas, Time of Your Life would not prove to be the time of anyone's life, actors and audiences alike. It soon went the way of other disastrous spin-offs, ones that began circling the drain from the very moment they hit the air.

During this hazy television gray period, she was cast in and worked on the filming of the stoner comedy, Dude, Where's My Car?. In the film, Jennifer plays Wanda, twin sister of Wilma (played by Marla Sokoloff). The twins are dating Jesse (Ashton Kutcher) and Chester (Seann William Scott), two incurable stoners who, after a twenty-four-hour bender, have managed to lose Jesse's car. Safely tucked in the car, or so Jesse and Chester believe, are the anniversary presents the guys had bought for the twins.

JENNIFER IS ADORABLY PRISSY, AND DESPITE THE SILLINESS OF THE FILM, THE ROLE DEFINITELY GOT HER NOTICED.

Next, in a huge departure from a delightfully inane teen film, she got signed for a small part in the testosterone-addled Pearl Harbor flop. She played a nerdy nurse in a role hardly as significant as Wanda in Dude, Where's My Car?.

It was a guy film after all. And as a result, it was also a completely male-dominated set. Jennifer remembers with glee for Movieline.com how the few girls cast in the film would cope with the masculine-driven madness: "We'd all gather...and play Madonna's

JENNIFER'S PROFESSIONAL PITFALLS AND ACHIEVEMENTS IN THIS PERIOD COULDN'T HOLD A CANDLE TO THE SURGE IN HER ROMANTIC LIFE.

Immaculate Collection and wear grass skirts and coconut bras and dance and make each other laugh," she smiled.

It was also in this time of her life that she would meet and eventually marry the love of her life, actor Scott Foley.

SYDNEY BRISTOW Living?

Can you imagine Sydney Bristow puttering around in the kitchen, complete with shocking red wig, rubber dress, and stiletto heels, perhaps following a recipe being played on a video she taped from her favorite show, Martha Stewart, Living? It's not likely. But then again, Jennifer Garner is not really Sydney Bristow. And what she loves more than anything else is to be at home, puttering away.

"I love Martha Stewart," Jennifer gushed in an Entertainment Tonight interview. "I know she's supposed to be mean, but I love her, I have her on my TIVO."

Part of Jennifer's secret for looking so svelte is that she's very careful about what she puts into her body. "You know, when we were doing the pilot, it was so important for me to eat my own food, so I would cook all of my meals for the week on Sunday—just have a big cook-a-thon and make all of these healthy things, such as chicken breast, a bunch of salads, maybe some vegetable lasagnas."

Could there be a new spin on a cooking show here?

JENNIFER vs. SYDNEY

How much like her Alias character Sydney Bristow is Jennifer Garner? "She is very lonely. She's an overachiever who works to the best of her abilities but can't believe she is in a position of not wanting to be a spy anymore," said Jennifer to Time magazine. Okay—overachiever we get, but the other two? Nope, doesn't quite sound like our girl. Let's compare the two ...

Jennifer

Sydney

Jennifer	Sydney
◎ HAPPY, UNEVENTFUL, AND NURTURING CHILDHOOD WITH TWO SOLID, TOGETHER, AND LOVING PARENTS.	◎ TUMULTUOUS CHILDHOOD WITH AN ENIGMATIC FATHER AND A MOTHER WHO DIED LONG BEFORE (OR SO WE ARE LEAD—OR MISLEAD—TO BELIEVE) SYDNEY WOULD KNOW HER SECRETS.
◎ FATHER IS AN ENGINEER.	◎ FATHER IS AN AGENT FOR A SUBVERSIVE SPY ORGANIZATION.
◎ MOTHER IS A PROFESSOR.	◎ MOTHER WAS A KGB SPY.
◎ HAPPILY MARRIED TO THE LOVE OF HER LIFE.	◎ FIANCÉ SHOT DEAD IN THE BATHTUB FOR KNOWING TOO MUCH. WILL SHE EVER FIND TRUE LOVE AGAIN?
◎ WEARS T-SHIRTS AND CARGO PANTS AND SNEAKERS AND NEVER WEARS MAKEUP UNLESS ITS ABSOLUTELY NECESSARY.	◎ WEARS OUTRAGEOUS WIGS AND GOWNS AND MANOLO BLAHNIK STILETTOS.
◎ IN CONTROL OF HER LIFE AND CAREER AND DESTINY; ONLY DOES WHAT SHE WANTS TO DO.	◎ IS FOREVER BEING PULLED IN BY HER CAREER AND HAS NO CONTROL OF HER DESTINY; DOESN'T KNOW IF SHE'LL EVER GET OUT AND HAVE A NORMAL LIFE.

TEST YOUR JENNIFER IQ
PART THREE

CONGRATULATIONS AGENT-IN-TRAINING.
YOU HAVE AT LAST MADE IT TO LEVEL 3—
YOU'RE MORE THAN HALFWAY ON YOUR WAY
TO BECOMING INTERNATIONAL WOMAN OF
MYSTERY! HOW MUCH DO YOU KNOW ABOUT
JENNIFER'S HOT AND COLD CAREER MOVES
THAT FINALLY ENDED HER UP IN FULL
COMMAND OF J.J. ABRAMS'S ATTENTION
AND IMAGINATION? ANSWER THE FOLLOWING
QUESTIONS TO FIND OUT. AND WHEN YOU'RE
DONE WITH THE QUIZ, BE SURE TO TURN TO
THE BACK OF THE BOOK AND WRITE IN
YOUR SCORE. GODSPEED!

1) What does Jennifer pack for lunch when she goes to work?
    a. plenty of junk food—the more Doritos, the better!
    b. baloney sandwiches on white bread—a staple of her childhood
    c. vegetable lasagna and healthy salads—right from her own kitchen
    d. pizza! pizza! pizza!—and the more toppings the better! A girl's got to keep up her strength after all!

2) Which famous music diva's tunes kept the girls occupied and sane between takes of Pearl Harbor?
    a. Mariah Carey
    b. Madonna
    c. Celine Dion
    d. Tina Turner

3) Who played Jennifer's twin sister in Dude, Where's My Car?
    a. Sarah Michelle Gellar
    b. Jessica Alba
    c. Marla Sokoloff
    d. Jennifer Love Hewitt

4) Which famed TV creative team brought Jennifer in for two projects in two years?
    a. Abrams and Andrews
    b. Littman and Keyser
    c. Sonny and Cher
    d. Donnie and Marie

5) What was Jennifer Garner's character's name in Time of Your Life?
    a. Wanda
    b. Randy
    c. Toni
    d. Romy

A.K.A. JENNIFER GARNER

THE UNAUTHORIZED BIOGRAPHY OF
AMERICA'S HOTTEST NEW STAR

LOVE AT LAST

CHAPTER FOUR

"SHE'S BEAUTIFUL IN A VERY FAMILIAR, ADORABLE WAY—YOU JUST CAN'T STOP WATCHING HER"

—J.J. ABRAMS ABOUT HIS STAR, TO ENTERTAINMENT WEEKLY

It was a Hollywood dream: Their eyes locked across a crowded and bustling set. They were cast to play old flames. They sized each other up wondering if the chemistry was going to be right—and if it would translate to audiences.

SOMEHOW JUST THE SIGHT OF THE OTHER MADE EACH WANT TO MELT. A SURGE OF ELECTRICITY SURGED BETWEEN THEM, EVEN AS THEY WERE YARDS AWAY FROM EACH OTHER. AND ONCE THEY FINALLY MET, THEY HAD AN INSTANT REPOIRE— AN INSTANT FLIRTATION. IT WAS AS IF THEY HAD ALWAYS KNOWN EACH OTHER...

Okay, so maybe this scenario is more like a script in the works, but it wasn't that far off from the actual events of when Jennifer Garner and her now-husband Scott Foley met working on Felicity together. "It was love at first sight," Jennifer told Seventeen magazine. And Scott would certainly agree.

It is true that Jennifer and Scott were fast friends during the filming of that first episode of Felicity. The magic was in the air and was obvious to everyone. It was the kind of pull that could make two more impetuous individuals decide to take off for Vegas two weeks after meeting and get hitched. But neither Jennifer nor Scott is programmed that way. So they took their time and let the relationship grow and develop while the romance blossomed.

"It was sweet and slow," Jennifer gushed to Seventeen. "I think we all grow up with the fear that we're going to lose the guy or he won't like us, so we overcompensate. It was different with Scott. For the first time I wasn't afraid."

Over the course of a few short months, they fell deliciously and completely in love. They took walks. Went to the park. They just spent time together, talking and getting to know one another. It took weeks before they even shared their first kiss. Well, their first kiss as just Scott and Jennifer that is. There was plenty of kissing on the show after all! As Jennifer giggled to Rolling Stone, "He didn't even kiss me until we'd been doing this for several weeks and we'd already taken our shirts off and made out on the show."

And then Scott made a big move: he invited Jennifer to Paris for New Year's Eve. Jennifer was a bit freaked out—not for herself per se, but because she was worried what her parents would think.

BUT IT DIDN'T SEEM TO MATTER TO ANYONE, BECAUSE ANYONE WHO KNEW JENNIFER AND SCOTT KNEW THEY WERE GOING TO END UP TOGETHER. IT WAS OBVIOUS.

"We rode the Ferris wheel, held hands, sipped hot chocolate in bistros," she told Seventeen, "and fell completely and ridiculously in love."

They got engaged, and on October 19, 2000, they made it official and got married.

As if this wasn't reason enough to cherish her stints on Felicity, it turned out that her guest role would turn out to be serendipitous on many levels. Not only would it be the channel through which she realized her romantic dreams, it was also, in a less straightforward way perhaps, the vehicle that would drive her to stardom.

WARNING!
HIGHLY CLASSIFIED
DOCUMENTATION

SCOTT FOLEY

MEET SCOTT FOLEY

When Scott met Jennifer on the Felicity set, he was blown away. Smitten might be too light a word. The chemistry was incredible—it was intense, yet comfortable. "She's me in female form," he has said of his beloved. "Not to sound cheesy, but Jennifer and I make 'one' really well."

And he's not far off with that statement, though his childhood was considerably more tumultuous than hers. Because his father worked in international banking, his family moved around a lot when he was growing up. But, like Jennifer, Scott is also one of three kids: three boys!

Professionally speaking, Scott and Jennifer are cut from the same cloth. Like Jennifer, Scott realized from a very early age that acting was all he wanted to do. When he was nine, he auditioned for a school play and clinched the part. From that point on, he devoted all of his energy to the honing of his craft.

Unlike Jennifer, Scott never considered college. After high school, he packed his bags and moved to California, determined to make it big. It would take years before he got a break, but he never gave up. He made ends meet with odd jobs—even selling cookies at Mrs. Field's—before he finally got a break. Scott's agent got him an audition for Dawson's Creek, and for several episodes, though he was never a regular, he played football-playing BMOC, Chip. This led him to the audition that made him a household name.

Scott was really impressed by the Felicity script, and saw himself as the obvious choice to play "Noel." The producers thought differently and cast him as "Ben". Fortunately, at what was practically the last minute, they found their Noel—and then realized that Scott Speedman would make a much better Ben. So Scott became Noel. Which, in the scheme of the universe,

HE MAN WHO STOLE
ENNIFER GARNER'S
RT, SCOTT FOLEY.

proved to be a very good thing. After all, it wasn't
Ben's ex-girlfriend that Jennifer was hired to play!
Felicity helped Scott's career take off. He has since
been cast in several roles for various films, including
Scream 3 and Rennie's Landing—in which Jennifer

SCOTT AND JENNIFER MAKE
UP ONE OF HOLLYWOOD'S
HOTTEST COUPLES

also has a small part. And not to mention, that without Felicity, he might
never have met his soul mate.

HOLLYWOOD COUPLES THAT WORK— AND KEEP WORKING

cou·ple (kŭp'əl) n.
1.   Two items of the same kind; a pair.
2.   Something that joins or connects two things together; a link.
3.   (used with a sing. or pl. verb)
a.   Two people united, as by betrothal or marriage.
b.   Two people together.
4.   Informal. A few; several: a couple of days.
5.   Physics. A pair of forces of equal magnitude acting in parallel but opposite directions, capable of causing rotation but not translation.

Hollywood is a notorious breeding ground for impulsive marriages between stars with, well, stars in their eyes. The average marriage between Hollywood celebrities usually lasts less than five years—if even that long. Sometimes one's career plummets while the other's soars. And sometimes a new star puts those stars back in one of their eyes. But it's not always like that. Some celebrity couples have been really lucky because each wants to be a part of the relationship and works hard to make it work. One look at Jennifer and Scott together and it's hard not to see that they have what it takes. What are some other success stories?

Reese Witherspoon and Ryan Phillippe

Reese and Ryan met for the first time when they worked together on the film Cruel Intentions. It was love at first sight. And while the two actors were decidedly young when they decided to wed in 1999, (she was 23; he 25), they have proven that when it's right, you just know. It doesn't matter how old you are.

Will Smith and Jada Pinkett Smith

Will and Jada met when she auditioned for his TV show, The Fresh Prince of Bel-Air. She was trying out for a part as Will's girlfriend. She didn't get it, for one because casting thought she was too short for him— but also because they believed there just wasn't the right chemistry between the two of them! Years later, Will and Jada are one of the most outwardly happy and sickeningly cute couples in Hollywood, even dressing in matching costumes and wild outfits to attend premieres.

Matthew Broderick and Sarah Jessica Parker

Married in a secret ceremony on May 19, 1997, Sarah Jessica Parker met Matthew Broderick when she was coming out of a short, intense romance with John F. Kennedy, Jr. Prior to that, she had a long-term relationship with Hollywood's favorite bad boy, Robert Downey, Jr. Broderick was coming out of a long-term relationship with Ferris Bueller co-star Jennifer Gray. They were firmly in love after working together in How to Succeed in Business Without Even Trying, and both have been thriving together—both in their relationships and their careers. She as the household-name Carrie in Sex in the City, he playing opposite Nathan Lane in the Broadway smash, The Producers.

Brad Pitt and Jennifer Aniston

Brad Pitt and Jennifer Aniston are the hands-down darlings of Hollywood couples, nearly of all time. For one, they are certainly two of the best-looking actors to ever grace stage or screen, but they are also alike in a more significant way: According to anyone who knows them, Brad and Jennifer are really down to earth people—which is a great foundation for their relationship.

Will Jennifer and Scott stand the test of time? One only needs to see how they support and care for each other now to see that it's the real thing. They are both stars on the rise, and even now, while she's racing ahead of him—and perhaps just for now—his enthusiasm about her and her career is truly genuine. "You know, it's the sweetest thing in the world," Jennifer gushed during an interview with *Entertainment Weekly*. "He's watched [*Alias*] literally 20 times. He will stop anyone on the street and say 'Have you seen my wife's show?' He's so proud of it, and it means so much to me I can't describe [it]."

OFFICIAL UNIFORM GUIDELINES

JENNIFER STYLE

> "SHE'S EVERYTHING YOU HOPE FOR IN THE STAR OF YOUR SHOW AND ONE OF THE STARS OF YOUR NETWORK."
> —LLOYD BRAUN, ABC ENTERTAINMENT COCHAIRMAN TO *ENTERTAINMENT WEEKLY.*

Jennifer Garner has a style all her own. She is the prototypical all-American girl, but somehow, in character, she pulls off the most outrageous looks gorgeously. And when she's all decked out for award shows and premieres—look out! Jennifer can slide from casual chic to glam chick faster than Wonder Woman can complete three spins—and just as effortlessly!

CASUAL

This is Jennifer's most prized look. When the weather's cold, it usually entails a comfy, relaxed-fit pair of jeans and a stretched-out oversized sweater to wrap herself up in. When the days get warmer, the jeans might get traded in for Capri pants and the sweater-a T-shirt, naturally. In either climate, it's more than likely that Jennifer will be wearing a worn-well pair of comfy sneakers on those tootsies!

It's also a safe bet that her hair will hang straight down without fuss, or in a simple ponytail, and that she'll probably not wear any makeup at all. Why would she need to with that flawless skin anyway! Perhaps just a slight gloss over her fabulous lips, and out the door she goes, ready to embrace the day.

> JENNIFER'S GORGEOUS LIPS HAVE BECOME THE TALK OF THE TOWN IN HOLLYWOOD. HERE, TONED DOWN IN CASUAL DRESS, SHE GIVES A PURSED SMILE AT A PARTY FOR MOTOROLA.

FORMAL

Jennifer kicks butt when she dresses for a night on the town. Because of her skin and hair coloring, red is the most flattering color she dons—as evidence by her striking appearance at the 59th Annual Golden Globes ceremony.

No matter the occasion, her dress style is always simple—no frills, baubles, or racy cuts for this natural beauty. The gorgeous tank-style gown she wore for the Globes stood alone without any trims, beads, or anything along those lines. And jewelry is hardly needed on Jennifer. A simple diamond bracelet and wedding band were all that was needed to brighten up the outfit. And Jennifer required no earrings at all, even though her hair was pulled back in a simple ponytail.

Jennifer's formal look is the only time she indulges in makeup—and even then, it's never overstated or overdone. Even in full makeup, Jennifer's look is natural. She uses browns and pinks to bring out her eyes and never in excess. Her cheekbones, already exquisitely carved into her face, could stand alone without blush—though a soft pinkish-brown brings more life to her face.

But perhaps the most outstanding feature of Jennifer's face are her full lips. No collagen implants, here, girls. Jennifer's lips have surpassed Julia Roberts' as the most sought-after in all of Hollywood (from the plastic surgeons, that is). Lots of bright lipstick would never do the trick. All she needs is a simple gloss and voila! Perfection!

THE DRESSED UP JENNIFER GARNER—GORGEOUS, YET STILL VERY NATURAL.

TEST YOUR JENNIFER IQ
PART FOUR

You're getting closer and closer to the home stretch—don't lose your cool now! If you are a fan of romance, this might be your favorite quiz of all. How much do you know about the romance of Scott Foley and Jennifer Garner? Take this quiz to find out! And don't forget to go to the back of the book to record your score!

1. What show was Jennifer working on when she met Scott Foley?
   a. Dawson's Creek
   b. Time of Your Life
   c. The Gillmore Girls
   d. Felicty

2. For which holiday did Scott take his future wife to Paris?
   a. her birthday
   b. New Year's Eve
   c. Groundhog Day
   d. Thanksgiving

3. What was the actual date that Scott and Jennifer became husband and wife?
   a. April 19, 2000
   b. May 4, 2001
   c. October 19, 2000
   d. October 19, 2001

4. In how many episodes of Felicity did Jennifer portray Hanna?
   a. one
   b. two
   c. four
   d. twelve

5. What is the name of the film Scott starred in, in which Jennifer played a minor role?
   a. Scream 3
   b. The Fast and the Furious
   c. Rennie's Landing
   d. Cruel Intentions

A.K.A. JENNIFER GARNER

THE UNAUTHORIZED BIOGRAPHY OF
AMERICA'S HOTTEST NEW STAR

THE ULTIMATE
BOND GIRL

CHAPTER FIVE

"THANK GOODNESS I LOVE MY JOB."

—JENNIFER GARNER TO *USA TODAY.*

If you're not familiar with the story of Sydney Bristow and the general gist of Alias, you've probably been living under a rock somewhere for the past year or so. But just in case you have, here's how it goes in a pretty condensed nutshell.

Grad student Sydney Bristow gets approached by who she thinks is the CIA to become an agent. What she eventually learns is that the agency that approached her was not in fact the CIA, but the SD-6, a subversive agency that in no way has the real CIA's interests at heart. When Sydney finds out that she's been duped, she enlists with the real CIA and becomes a double agent to help bring the SD-6 down.

In the process, she becomes entangled with her estranged father. Her fiancé is murdered in the bathtub when SD-6 finds out that he knows what his wife-to-be does for a living. She keeps her two closest friends—a guy friend who's in love with her and her own roommate—purposely and effectively in the dark about what she does—they think she's in banking. She learns that her dead mother was a KGB agent—and that she might not even be dead at all. And she has a mega-crush on her CIA handler. Breathe. Scratch scalp. Sigh.

Sounds like a lot, but that's only the tip of the iceberg.

PART OF THE POPULARITY OF THE SHOW IS CERTAINLY THE COMPLEXITY OF THE PLOT LINES, WHICH PEOPLE ARE SOMETIMES TOO CONFUSED TO FOLLOW. BUT IT MATTERS NOT.

"You don't have to get the plot to like the show," Jennifer Garner explained to USA Today. "People are intimidated by the idea that it's confusing. It's not that confusing. If you don't care about the mission, you can watch it simply for the wigs and dresses, and then focus on the emotional parts, because that's what the show is about." Which is a relief for those who don't want to do that much thinking at the end of the weekend!

"It's not an action show," Jennifer continued. "The action is a byproduct of the story, which is this girl who is in a muddle, and the only way she can get out is to be something she hates, a double agent.

When what all she really wants is to kiss the guy and have a dad."

That the show can fly back and forth between its many complex identities as a show is certainly part of the magic.

THE PLOT SURPRISES KEEP VIEWERS ON THEIR TOES — AND THEY ARE EFFECTIVELY AND PURPOSELY KEPT AS JUST THAT: SURPRISES. IN FACT, NOT EVEN CAST MEMBERS ARE ALLOWED TO KNOW WHAT'S GOING TO HAPPEN FROM WEEK TO WEEK.

Or so some of them, like Jennifer, would lead you to believe.

In a recent Entertainment Weekly interview, Jennifer was feeling particularly mischievous and playful for reporter Dan Snierson. He wanted to know: Did she know what her character was going to be doing from one week to the next? She had fun with him by relaying a cloak-and-dagger mission she made to the writers' room one day. She snuck in when no one was looking, and read all the story ideas pasted on the wall. "And when I started to leave the room," she told him, "I heard a toilet flush in the bathroom across the way and somebody started to walk out." And then she slipped into full Sydney Bristow mode, like Clark Kent ducking into a phone booth. "So I full-on swept back around and had my back against the wall and hide there, listening out the door, not even breathing," she continued, "and waiting for the person to walk down the hall. And before they'd turned the corner, I was down the hall and out of the way. And I was so excited about pulling a spy move that I forgot everything that I'd read."

Later he would find out that she did know more than she had let

Michael Vartan

Bradley Cooper

Jennifer accepted the People's Choice Award on behalf of the show, flanked by co-stars.

on, and had just been yanking his chain. And that's another side of Jennifer: under that well-toned, Christian good girl façade lurks the heart of a sprightly devil. When confronted, she laughed for Snierson. "...I told you with a wink in my voice," she smiled.

It was a blessing in disguise that Jennifer hadn't yet had a huge breakthrough role when she was signed on to play Sydney Bristow in Alias.

They say that timing is everything, and nothing could be truer

AS AN ACTRESS, SHE WAS JUST EXPERIENCED ENOUGH TO BRING DEPTH AND DIMENSION TO THE CHARACTER, AND JUST FRESH ENOUGH IN THE EYES OF THE PUBLIC TO PULL OFF THE ROLE WITHOUT PREJUDICE FROM AUDIENCE AND CRITICS.

than that when it comes to Jennifer's success with Alias.

But there was a time when it might not have been Jennifer Garner's role to play. Sure, J.J. Abrams had thought of her when he developed the show, but he didn't have the absolute and final say on who his latest leading lady was going to be. But he was going to try his damnedest to make sure it happened to be Jennifer. He hadn't worked with her that much, but he believed in her.

"There was something about her that I just thought was really special," he told USA Today. "I always thought she had something in her personality that was funnier and sexier and smarter and more mischievous than anything I'd seen her do. And when I wrote Sydney, I wanted to show that."

And when you feel something so strongly, it's hard to contain that enthusiasm.

Jennifer's talent was undeniable; he was confident that that could

HE WANTED TO GRAB UP JENNIFER RIGHT ON THE SPOT BEFORE SHE FOUND SOMETHING BIGGER AND BETTER WITH WHICH TO FILL HER DANCE CARD.

happen at any moment. So he tipped her off.

Jennifer was more than thrilled to say the least. She was wondering what her next big project was going to be, and "Then J.J.

[Abrams] put a bug in my ear, telling me he was writing this show," she told Rolling Stone.

The prospect was so exciting because it was unlike anything she had ever done before. But she could adapt. She knew she could. And she was ripe for the challenge. "I really loved the Charlie's Angels movie," she said, "and seeing it really made me want to do something physical."

Now Jennifer always prided herself on keeping her body in shape. She is a former dancer, after all, not to mention all the other athletic activities she had pursued growing up. Indeed, these early activities had primed Jennifer's body to be able to develop the strength to pull off what she would demand of it for her work in Alias. But certainly, in all of her athletic pursuits, martial arts had not exactly been a part of her regimen. No matter.

JENNIFER ACCEPTED THE CHALLENGE LIKE SHE DID ANY OTHER CHALLENGE IN HER LIFE: WITH A LEVEL HEAD AND A FIRM GAME PLAN IN PLACE.

If she didn't know boo about martial arts, she wasn't going to fake it. That simply was not her style. So she took action.

As soon as she found out about the role, she knew she had about a month before she had to audition. So she whipped out the local phone directory and started calling around. She found an instructor she liked, and for the next month, she took classes religiously. It became her life.

Of course, like anything else, martial arts were a hard thing to master if you started it as late in life as she had. Not that she was old, per se, but her classmates were generally much, much younger. Most of them young enough to be her own children. And as is the way with kids, they picked it up like it was something they did every day, like walking; Jennifer took considerably more time. It was a riot.

Another person, a less strong and focused person, might have given up. But Jennifer was cool enough to see the humor. "...these five-year-olds would come in and run circles around me," she told Rolling Stone. "It was sad. But for some reason, I kept going. I loved adding violence to what I already knew how to do."

Finally, she started getting the moves down. And then it was time for her audition.

Jennifer auditioned and not everyone was as excited as Abrams about casting her as Sydney. "People said, 'She's an interesting choice,'" Abrams told Time magazine. But he stuck behind his star all the way. He knew that no other actress would be able to pull off Sydney as well as Jennifer.

Abrams was insistent. He would not give up on her. "I thought there was unlimited potential with Jennifer, like she could do anything," he told Entertainment Weekly. "She played a nerd in Pearl Harbor. When she was on Felicity, she was the nerdy girl with the glasses, the composer, the brain.... But I felt that she was Clark Kent. And I was dying to see her rip those glasses off and fly. It's like 'Who is she going to be?'" That belief of his finally paid off. Abrams was finally able to convince the big boys that Jennifer was born to play Sydney.

AT LAST JENNIFER CLINCHED THE ROLE. ALIAS WOULD GO INTO PRODUCTION, WITH JENNIFER LEADING THE STELLAR CAST.

Jennifer surrounded by fellow cast members Michael Vartan, Ron Rifkin, Kevin Weisman, and Victor Garber.

The first episode aired on September 28, 2001. It was ground-breaking television. Not only did it run for sixty-nine minutes, it ran without commercial interruption. Nikon had agreed to fully sponsor the entire block. Now folks could get totally immersed in the show and not lose their concentration on the plot.

It was an undeniable hit. Audiences were rapt. Critics were stunned. And for the most part, congratulatory. There were a few skeptics who didn't think that Alias could maintain its momentum after the first episode, however. Variety's Phil Gallo wondered after watching the second episode: "If this is a sign of its direction, one wonders how long it will be before Bristow is captured by a Penguin-like villain and dunked in a cake made of quicksand, like Batman when Adam West wore the tights and cape."

Just as wrapping up of the first season was going on, most everyone who had ever been doubtful had been converted.

"This is the only new show of the season that I watch," Quentin

AUDIENCES ARE WILD ABOUT SYDNEY, AND EVEN FOLKS IN THE BUSINESS CAN'T HELP BUT TOSS A CONGRATULATORY NOD ITS WAY.

Jennifer strikes a pose.

Tarantino told Rolling Stone. "Alias delivers what The Man From U.N.C.L.E always promised: it actually lives up to the coolness of its potential."

Jennifer is ecstatic about the success of the show, but anything that good can be very demanding. "I have to be very strong to play this character," she told Seventeen. "If I'm not, I'll get hurt." So what exactly does that entail?

Jennifer's week is hectic to say the very least. Her typical day starts at 4:00AM. She kickboxes. She works out. She runs. And then it's off to work for days that sometimes run fifteen hours long.

Weekends are reserved for interviews— and of course there's all that cooking she does on Sundays! Not to mention spending time with Scott and their two dogs. The woman barely has time to breathe.

But the results have been well worth the work.

JENNIFER HAS A ROCK HARD BODY THAT JUST WON'T QUIT. AND HER NEW PHYSICAL STRENGTH TRANSLATES TO MANY DIFFERENT LEVELS.

"It feels great to be physical," she told Seventeen magazine. "I'm much braver than I used to be."

So with all the martial arts training she's had in recent months to become Sydney, can she hold her own in a fight? She doubts it. "OK, I know my punches aren't good enough to hurt anyone... God, I hope they don't think I'm Sydney."

But there's another side effect of playing such a physically demanding role. Jennifer comes home each and every day mottled with black and blue marks. It was so bad once, in fact, that when she went to the doctor on an unrelated matter—just a checkup really—the nurse started talking to her about services available for women who were being battered by their husbands. Obviously she had never seen the show! "I don't mind getting bruises," laughed Jennifer to Rolling Stone, "they make me feel tough."

Jennifer Garner was absolutely stunning in the red gown she wore for the Golden Globes.

Of course, not everyone shares her enthusiasm—least of all the suspected wife beater, Scott. "I'm bruised a lot. I'll get out of the shower and I'll be like, 'Scott, look!' He's just so horrified," she told Rolling Stone. "He's like, 'I have no interest in your bruises. I don't think it's funny. I don't think it's cool.'"

But Jennifer would not have it any other way. She wants to be as involved in her character as is physically possible. "Part of what's cool about the show is that it's authentic," she told Entertainment Weekly. "If you look, I'm doing it. And part of what's cool about playing this character is getting pushed in that way. So whenever it gets tough, to suddenly say, 'No, I don't want to do it'—that's not really being this girl. So I'm totally 100 percent committed to doing everything I possibly can."

BUT IF THERE'S SOMETHING THAT RIVALS THE BRUISES IN THE ODDNESS JENNIFER FEELS AT PORTRAYING THIS CHARACTER, IT'S THE OUTFITS.

They're a lot for a conservative small-town girl to pull off—both physically and emotionally. She has admitted on more than one occasion how she blushes pink every time she puts one of the outrageous costumes on. "Omigosh, I'm so embarrassed having to wear those dresses on the set," she blushed to Rolling Stone. "I just have to tell myself, 'It's not me out there, it's a character, and if she has to dress like a slut, so be it.'" But remember—there are many sides of Jennifer. Never forget the mischievous side. Ever. At the end of this statement, Jennifer coyly added: "Anyway, that's what I tell my dad." What does she tell her husband? He surely must have just the slightest notion that half the nation is in total love with his wife—both for her acting chops but for those drop-dead looks and a body that just won't quit.

Despite the demure front she projects, Jennifer actually really likes the outfits. "After the parachuting stunt, I ripped off my clothes like Britney Spears and exposed this fierce dress underneath. I get embarrassed wearing the sexy outfits," she admitted to Seventeen magazine. "Sydney's clothes are more va-va-voom than I'm used to. But it's fun to have permission to wear that stuff."

When she's on break from Alias, she'd like to pursue more film

FOR THE TIME BEING, ALIAS IS REALLY JENNIFER'S WHOLE LIFE. HER PLANS FOR THE RECENT FUTURE INCLUDE WORKING, WORKING, AND, WELL, WORKING.

roles. It's the pragmatist in her, really. "I've spent plenty of time unemployed," she told Seventeen, "it's my time to work now."

Jennifer and Scott are both looking forward to the day when they can start a family—but these plans are on hold for the far future. All in time. No matter how bad-ass Sydney Bristow is, it would be pretty inconceivable for her to perform all those acrobatic feats carrying all that mass at front. And they don't really make those sexy designer outfits in maternity styles, do they?

Jennifer's crowning moment as an actress to date came when she swooped the Golden Globe in the 2002 ceremony—and right out from under such established actresses as Lorraine Braco, Edie Falco (both nominated for The Sopranos), and Amy Brenneman (Judging Amy). "To say that I was surprised and shocked would be the understatement of the century—of the millennium," she told Hollywood Reporter about clinching the statue. "It's a good start, don't you think?"

And now the next question that everyone suspects will be on Jennifer's lips:

DUDE, WHERE'S MY EMMY?!?

Jennifer is a woman of many, many expressions—but no one can deny the excitement and joy radiating off her face after she clinched the Golden Globe award.

MEET J.J. ABRAMS

THE other MAN IN JENNIFER'S LIFE

If there's one name to pin on J.J. Abrams, it would have to be "Mr. Creativity."

Either that, or "Mr. Energy."

Not only did he dream up Alias and write it, he is also the show's executive producer, the composer of the theme music—even the designer of the opening credits. Visionary. Businessman. Graphic designer.

But his creativity and energy is not exclusive to his work. It carries over in other aspects of his life as well. For example, on Valentine's Day, it wasn't enough to simply buy his wife a box of candy. He actually made her a chocolate bar, designing and implementing the mold; pouring the chocolate and waiting for it to harden. Then he packed it in one of his famous handmade boxes.

Not many screenwriters can boast their first film credit as a major Hollywood production. Not, of course, unless they are J.J. Abrams, creator of the

WB's Felicity and Jennifer's star-making ABC show, Alias. In 1990, Abrams co-wrote, with Jill Mazursky, Taking Care of Business—a film that starred Charles Grodin and James Belushi.

His first solo effort came in 1991. It was Regarding Henry, the story of a ruthless, cutthroat lawyer who gets shot. During his recovery from the ensuing brain damage, he comes back to the man that he used to be before being driven mad by power. Harrison Ford played the title role.

Abrams scripts always seem to attract some of the biggest names in Hollywood. In 1992, Forever Young, the story of a pilot who is cryogenically frozen for fifty years when he misbelieves that his beloved has been squashed by a car and killed, featured Mel Gibson, Jamie Lee Curtis, and Elijah Wood.

In the mid to late 1990s, Abrams films took a comic bent, and this time he was able to attract "Ross" and "Rachel" as leads. In 1996, The Pallbearer became actor David Schwimmer's first leading man role; in 1997, Picture Perfect brought Jennifer Anniston back to the big screen.

And then, in 1998, Abrams, with long-time collaborator and pal Matt Reeves, moved his vision to the small screen and introduced the world to Felicity, a quasi-flaky student who chooses a college to be closer to her high school crush—a boy who didn't even know her name in high school. With its complex yet sweet relationship issues and angst, Felicity became a huge hit.

One day, in a story idea meeting, Abrams was fretting because he couldn't come up with a new premise for Felicity one week. He remembered the inspiration for Rolling Stone magazine: "You know what would be amazing? If Felicity were recruited by the C.I.A. and sent on all these crazy kick-ass missions, and when she came back she couldn't tell anyone about what she was doing."

And Alias was born.

Could the same man who created Felicity pull off a spy drama with equal gusto? J.J. Abrams knew he could pull it off without a hitch.

"It just happens to be told in this weird amalgam of genres," he told Entertainment Weekly. "And it truly is an amalgam. I love comedies, I love romantic comedies, I love dramas, I love romantic dramas, I love science fiction films, I love thrillers. When I wrote Alias, I decided, 'Screw it, I'm going to write something that has everything I love.'"

J.J. ABRAMS BODY OF WORK

2001
ALIAS (CREATOR, WRITER, PRODUCER)

1999
THE SUBURBANS (ACTOR)

1998
FELICITY (CO-CREATOR, CO-WRITER,
CO-EXECUTIVE PRODUCER)
ARMAGEDDON (WRITER)

1996
THE PALLBEARER (PRODUCER, WRITER)

1993
SIX DEGREES OF SEPARATION (ACTOR)

1992
FOREVER YOUNG (WRITER)

1991
REGARDING HENRY (WRITER)

1990
TAKING CARE OF BUSINESS (CO-WRITER)

WHO'S WHO IN THE CAST OF ALIAS?

Part of what makes Alias such a great show is the writing, of course. But without the right mix of actors to fill the roles with incredible chemistry and believability, the lines would be just that: one-dimensional words on paper. Here's an insight into the talents that play off Jennifer so well and make the show attract more and more viewers with each and every episode. Of her costars Jennifer told USA Today: "It's not like I just appreciate them; I revere them." And they her.

"There are times when you're acting in a scene with her, and even when the camera's on you, all of a sudden, you just kind of lose yourself in her. And you're just like, 'Oh wow,'" co-star Michael Vartan told Entertainment Weekly. "I don't want to make it sound like this crazy, intense thing, but she just sucks you in and you can't help it. I mean, she's so beautiful but she's so vulnerable. She's just this puppy.... All right, could we be any more in love with her? Seriously. Is that possible?"

The creators and cast of Alias pose after they clinched the People's Choice Award for Favorite New Dramatic Series in January 2002.

Victor Garber (Jack Bristow)

Canadian-born character actor Victor Garber has performed his way through memorable stage, screen, and television roles since be began his career at the age of ten, doing community theater in his home-town of London, Ontario. He made his film debut portraying Jesus in the film version of the popular Broadway show Godspell in 1973, a role he played in the Toronto version of the musical. He has earned four Tony nominations and an Emmy nomination for his work in Life With Judy Garland: Me and My Shadows, and for a guest appearance on Frasier. He has played everything from Liberace in Liberace: Behind the Music to the lecherous Professor Callahan in Legally Blonde. A veritable chameleon of the thespian set, it's certainly no wonder he can pull off the role of Sydney's distant and duplicitous dad Jack Bristow as well as he does.

Michael Vartan (Agent Vaughn)

Michael Vartan was adorable in his role as Drew Barrymore's lanky love interest, Sam Coulsen, in Never Been Kissed. The Paris-born actor made his mark on the American movie scene in 1995 in To Wong Fu—Thanks for Everything Julie Newmar, and then again in 1996 in J.J. Abrams's The Pallbearer. And if that's not enough degrees of Hollywood separation, he also acted in The Curve with Felicity star Keri Russell in 1998.

Ron Rifkin (Arvin Sloane)

One of the most recognizable members of the Alias cast, actor Ron Rifkin has been in such films as Boiler Room, Keeping the Faith, and two Woody Allen films: Manhattan Murder Mystery and Husbands and Wives. In addition to film, he has done immeasurable amounts of theater—even winning a Best Supporting Tony Award for his work in Cabaret in 1998. On the small screen, he has guest-starred on Hill Street Blues, Falcon Crest, Law & Order, and ER.

Kevin Weisman (Marshall)

Marshall is Los Angeles born and bred Kevin Weisman's first major role. He has had extensive theater credits, and has made guest appearances on tons of shows, including Felicity (here we go again!), The X-Files, Just Shoot Me, and Frasier. He has had small parts in several films, including Gone in Sixty Seconds, and both produced and performed in The Illusion, a 2001 feature film directed by Michael Goorjian.

Carl Lumbly (Agent Dixon)

A theater veteran, Carl Lumbly has executed both dramatic and comedic parts with decided expertise.

His film credits include small roles in such films as The Bedroom Window, Pacific Heights, and How Stella Got Her Groove Back. On television, he's graced the sets of Cagney and Lacey, The West Wing, and The X-Files, and had a recurring role on ER.

Merrin Dungey (Francie)

Like Jennifer, Merrin Dungey is a former ballerina who only started acting seriously when she was in her late teens. She appeared in several television commercials, and after the success of her HBO one-woman show, Black Like Who?, she landed guest spots on several TV shows, including Friends and Murphy Brown, and had a recurring roles on Malcolm in the Middle and The King of Queens.

Bradley Cooper (Will Tippin)

A 1997 Georgetown graduate, Bradley Cooper moved to New York in 1997 to pursue a graduate degree in drama. But higher education would not be in the cards. He landed a guest spot on Sex in the City, and was soon hosting the Discovery Channel's Extreme Treks in a Wild World. His first feature film role was as Ben in Wet Hot American Summer in 2001, which starred Janeane Garofolo and David Hyde Pierce. He was cast in Darren Star's short-lived Fox drama The $treet, which also featured 2001 Golden Globe winner Jennifer Connelly.

TEST YOUR JENNIFER IQ
PART FIVE

Alright! You've made it pretty darn far, haven't you? This is your very last challenge. Up for it? Or are you getting tired and weak? There's only one way to find out now, isn't there? Rise to the occasion! And don't forget to record your score in the back!

1. How long had Jennifer been training in martial arts before her Alias audition?
    a. all her life
    b. twelve years
    c. one year
    d. one month

2. On what night did Alias first air?
    a. September 4, 2001
    b. September 8, 2001
    c. September 28, 2001
    d. September 6, 2002

3. Which electronics manufacturer sponsored the commercial-free first episode of Alias?
    a. Motorola
    b. Nikon
    c. Casio
    d. JVC

4. Which role does Victor Garber play on the show?
    a. Sydney's best guy pal, Marshall
    b. Sydney's dad, Jack
    c. Sydney's CIA handler, Agent Vaughn
    d. Sydney's roommate, Francie

5. Which of the following did J.J. Abrams not write:
    a. The screenplay for Armageddon
    b. The screenplay for Legally Blonde
    c. The screenplay for Regarding Henry
    d. The screenplay for Forever Young

TEST YOUR JENNIFER IQ ANSWER KEY

CHAPTER ONE
1) C
2) B
3) D
4) C
5) D

CHAPTER TWO
1) A
2) B
3) D
4) C
5) B

CHAPTER THREE
1) C
2) B
3) C
4) B
5) D

CHAPTER FOUR
1) D
2) B
3) C
4) B
5) C

CHAPTER FIVE
1) D
2) C
3) B
4) B
5) B

SECRET WORD DECODER MISSION

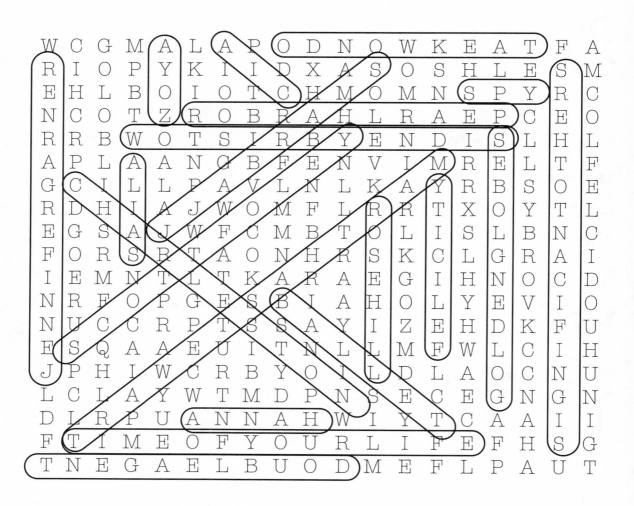

A/K/A: JENNIFER GARNER THE REAL STORY

HIDDEN WORDS

ALIAS
BALLET
CHARLESTON
CIA
DOUBLE AGENT
FELICITY
GOLDEN GLOBES
HANNA
JJ ABRAMS
JENNIFER GARNER

MARTHA STEWART
PEARL HARBOR
ROSE HILL
SCOTT FOLEY
SIDNEY BRISTOW
SIGNIFICANT
OTHERS
SPY
TAE KWON DO
TIME OF YOUR LIFE
ZOYA

Test Your Jennifer I.Q. Scoring Section

The moment of truth has arrived. How well do you really know Jennifer Garner? Is she right out in the open for you—or is she an enigma shrouded in mystery? Give yourself one point for each right answer. Then, follow these steps and see how you do!

1) List your points:

QUIZ NUMBER ONE   _____

QUIZ NUMBER TWO   _____

QUIZ NUMBER THREE   _____

QUIZ NUMBER FOUR   _____

QUIZ NUMBER FIVE   **+**   _____

_____

2) Add them up: Total score:

3) So... How'd you do?

0-10 POINTS

AND YOU CALL YOUR- SELF A FAN? WELL, GUESS WHAT? AS MUCH AS YOU LIKE JENNIFER AT THIS POINT, YOU REALLY DON'T KNOW THAT MUCH ABOUT HER AT ALL. SURE, YOU MIGHT KNOW THAT SHE ROCKS THE HOUSE AS SYDNEY BRISTOW, BUT HER PERSONAL LIFE MAY BE A BIG FOG TO YOU. NO WORRIES. RE-READ THE BOOK AND PORE THROUGH THE NEWS-STAND AND INTERNET FOR JENNIFER-RELATED STORIES. YOU'LL INCREASE YOUR JENNIFER I.Q. IN NO TIME, FLAT!

11-20 POINTS

IN THE MIDDLE GROUND. OKAY, SO YOU DON'T KNOW EVERYTHING THERE IS TO KNOW ABOUT JENNIFER GARNER—BUT YOU'RE GETTING THERE! WHY NOT CHECK OUT A FEW OF HER EARLY MOVIES, LIKE *MR. MAGOO* OR *DUDE, WHERE'S MY CAR?*. MAYBE YOU CAN DIG UP THE OLD EPISODES OF *FELICITY* IN WHICH SHE MADE THOSE TV PERFORMANCES THAT CAUGHT J.J. ABRAMS'S EYE!

A/K/A: JENNIFER GARNER THE REAL STORY

21-25 POINTS

You win the highest distinction for huge fan of Jennifer Garner. Scoring in this category—you really know your stuff! But don't get cocky, now! Jennifer is a star on the rise. Each and every day there's going to be new stuff to learn about her and new places in which to see her. Be sure to check out the **IMDb** (International Movie Database) website from time to time to see what new stuff she's going to be up to—or better yet, check out the Official Jennifer Garner website at WWW.JENNIFER-GARNER.COM.

JENNIFER GARNER: BODY OF WORK

FILMS

2002
Daredevil, **as Elektra**

2001
Rennie's Landing, **as Kylie Bradshaw**
Pearl Harbor, **as Lieutenant Sandra**
Dude, Where's My Car?, **as Wanda**

1998
1999, **as Annabell**

1997
In Harm's Way, **as Kelly**
Mr. Magoo, **as Stacey Sampanahoditra**
Washington Square, **as Marian Almond**
Deconstructing Harry, **as woman in elevator**

1996
Harvest of Fire, **as Sarah Troyer**

TELEVISION (MOVIES)

1999

Aftershock: Earthquake in New York, as Diane Agostini

1996

Rose Hill, as Mary Rose Clayborne Victoria Elliot at age 17
Dead Man's Walk, as Clara Forsythe

1995

Zoya, as Sasha

TELEVISION (PROGRAMS)

2001

Alias, as Sydney Bristow

1999

Time of Your Life, as Romy Sullivan

1998

Significant Others, as Nell Glennon

TELEVISION (GUEST APPEARANCES)

1998

Felicity, as Hannah (two episodes)
Fantasy Island, as Sally

1996

The Pretender, **as Billie H. Vaughn/Dupree**
Spin City, **as Becky**

1990

Law & Order **(unbilled)**

A/K/A: JENNIFER GARNER THE REAL STORY

BIBLIOGRAPHY

PERIODICALS

"A Woman We Love: Jennifer Garner." Esquire. June 2001.

Bianco, Robert. "Sydney Bristow in the Flesh." USA Today. February 1, 2002.

———. "The Plot Is Not the Point, But if You Need to Know it." USA Today. February 1, 2002.

Binelli, Mark. "Spy Girl: How 'Alias Star Jennifer Garner, a nice girl from the Bible Belt, Grew up to Become the Ass-Kickingest Babe on TV." Rolling Stone. February 14, 2002.

Fretts, Bruce. "Best Spy Chick: Jennifer Garner." Entertainment Weekly. December 21, 2001.

Gallo, Phil. "Alias (review)." Variety. October 1, 2001.

"Jennifer Garner." Hollywood Reporter. January 22, 2002.

Kelleher, Terry. "Significant Others (television program reviews)." People Weekly. March 16, 1998.

Luscombe, Belinda and Jeanne McDowell. "The Chick Who Kicks: Jennifer Garner is Chic, Sleek, and Geeky as TV's Most Delectable Double Agent. And She Kills." Time. February 4, 2002.

Rhein, Leslie. "Role Reversal (Get the Look): New Looks for Jennifer Garner and Rose McGowan." Teen Magazine. February 2002.

Richmond, Ray. "Time of Your Life (review)." Variety. October 25, 1999.

"Scene Stealers: Actress Jennifer Garner Sure Knows How to Stand Out." In Style. December 1, 2001.

Snierson, Dan. "Secrets & Spies." Entertainment Weekly. March 8, 2002.

Tucker, Ken. "Broad Appeal: With the Rock 'em, Sock 'em Action Drama Alias, Felicity Creator J.J. Abrams Finds Another Lady Who's A Champ." Entertainment Weekly. October 12, 2001.

. "Rose Hill." Entertainment Weekly. April 18, 1997.

. "Significant Others (television program reviews)." Entertainment Weekly. March 20, 1998.

. "Undercover Angel: A Mix of Heart-Stopping Plots, High-Octane Action, and an Emotional Kick is the Secret Formula Behind Alias." Entertainment Weekly. November 23, 2001.

Vaughan, Brendan. "A Woman We Love: Jennifer Garner." Esquire. March 2002.

Wycoff, Alice. "Secret Agent?" Seventeen. March 2002.

WORLD WIDE WEB

ABC online
Allmovie.com
Chicago Tribune online
E! online
Entertainment Tonight online
IMDb.com
Jennifer-Garner.com
Scottfoley.net
The U.S. Census Online
Zap2it.com

ABOUT THE AUTHOR

Maggie Marron is a New York-based freelance writer and editor who has profiled various celebrities for People magazine online. Maggie is the author of more than a dozen celebrity profile books, including Britney Spears: Stylin', Will Smith: From Rap Star to Mega Star, and *N Sync/N Depth.